GABO AND COLOUR

15 January - 27 March 2004

Annely Juda Fine Art
23 Dering Street (off New Bond Street)
London W1S 1AW
ajfa@annelyjudafineart.co.uk
www.annelyjudafineart.co.uk
Tel   020 7629 7578   Fax   020 7491 2139
Monday - Friday 10 - 6   Saturday 10 - 1

Cover: **Untitled** 1970s oil and pencil on paper, partly created with stencils

We would like to thank especially Nina and Graham Williams for making this exhibition possible and we would also like to thank Michael Harrison for his wonderful essay. We know he spent a lot of time talking to Nina who was able to give him so much information about her father's continual thoughts about the use of colour.

We are proud to be able to make this exhibition which we hope will help people to see an important and different aspect of Naum Gabo's work.

Annely and David Juda

1 **Column** 1975
glass, perspex and stainless steel
193 x 156 cm diameter

2 **Copy of the Realistic Manifesto** 1920
print on paper
62 x 78.5 cm

Gabo and Colour

'Thence in painting we renounce colour as a pictorial element, colour is the idealised optical surface of objects; an exterior and superficial expression of them; colour is accidental and it has nothing in common with the innermost essence of a thing.
We affirm that the tone of a substance, i.e., its light-absorbing material body, is its only pictorial reality.' [1]

'The Realistic Manifesto' does not bode well for an exhibition about colour and Naum Gabo whose work is most commonly typified by construction in colourless perspex and nylon.

His daughter, Nina, recalls a childhood in a house of natural materials and colours, where comic books were prohibited because of their colour, and Gabo treating her mother, Miriam, to an oatmeal suit and a brown-banded hat. This was the apparently austere aesthetic of the friend and admirer of Ben Nicholson, maker of white reliefs and painter of the most muted of palettes.

But palette there was in the sculptor's household, Miriam's paintbox which Gabo had annexed as his own almost from day one, insisting that every artist's home should have some paints. Around the lunch table there could be endless discussion of how to mix the colour of a particular rose or flower and one day he returned from Italy with a length of orange silk for a dress for Nina. Here was the admirer of Matisse, the colourist he estimated above all others who had changed the course of painting in the twentieth century.

More than forty years after 'The Realistic Manifesto' was published, Gabo determined to correct the impression that he had dismissed the use of colour out of hand. 'That is because in Russian there are two words for colour, and it is hard to translate. There is *Tsvet*, which is surface colour, or colour which reflects light, and there is *Faktura*, which is the depth of colour, or colour absorbing light.' [2] It was the former he had rejected, on the one hand the sham of illusionistic, academic painting but, on the other, the insistence on flatness and the attempt to eliminate colour's spatial qualities by the Suprematists and Mondrian, whom he saw as 'chasing windmills'. [3]

In the series of lectures he gave at the National Gallery of Art in Washington in 1959, [4] he high-lighted the importance of the Russian painter Mikhail Vrubel to himself and other artists of his generation. Vrubel (1856-1910) found 'the schematization of living nature, revolting'. Labelled as a 'decadent', he had bypassed the Russian art of the previous two centuries which under Western influence had become descriptive and disconnected from the common man in its service of the privileged classes. Before Peter the Great Russian art had been immune to the changes in style which had occurred in the West. Both its folk art and its ecclesiastical art, as Gabo saw them, combined in their abstract expression a spiritual and idealistic dimension with a utilitarian, social function. 'Detached from the crude realism of the material world', the icon or fresco painter 'did not need to look for inspiration to imitation of the material aspects of Nature', and his art was accessible to everybody. This was the tradition with which Vrubel had identified and 'toward the end of the nineteenth century we see a rebirth of those fundamental, idealistic, and abstract concepts which always prevailed in the whole previous history of Russian art.' Perversely, this would prepare the way for a reconnection with French painting: 'when, at the beginning of this century, many of us came into contact with Western European art, we did not come to a foreign land; we came back home, and Cézanne was accepted by us quite naturally. . . . Even Cubism was not entirely a surprise to us.'

Unlike his brother, Antoine Pevsner, Gabo had not been allowed to pursue his artistic ambitions from the outset and arrived as a sculptor only via the reluctant study of medicine, natural sciences and civil engineering. All three disciplines, coupled with an awareness of Cubism picked up in Paris where Antoine was painting and of Kandinsky's *Concerning The Spiritual in Art*, and added to the lack of an academic art training, were probably the ideal prelude for the revolutionary art of Constructivism. Cubism was to be rejected as still being concerned with the surface of things, Impressionism for its 'purely optical reflex',[5] and Futurism for its cumbersome attempts to convey mechanical speed when now we knew that light travelled at 300 km a second. Constructive art instead was to be built on 'the laws of life'. 'Space and time are the only forms on which life is built and hence art must be constructed.'[6]

Proclamations such as this have tended to lead to the equation of the constructive with the scientific, mathematical and purely logical. Here, after all, was the art of a new, rationally based, atheist, egalitarian society built with, as they became available, the synthetic materials of the modern age. But such constraints were never part of Gabo's vision.

In supposedly spurning colour the manifesto aspired to the realisation of 'the innermost essence of a thing' as opposed to a superficially perceived reality. Much later Gabo would explain that this was not to be found 'reflected on the retina'[7] nor by the scientist, 'separating himself from it and looking at it as an outsider. . . . The artist does not observe the world, he lives it.'[8] His job is to 'give an image to the experiences of our consciousness',[9] partaking of the totality of his faculties of feeling, senses and reason.

A deeply felt, intuitive response to colour was one such vital faculty. Colour would make a dramatic appearance in a sculpture such as *Linear Construction in Space No. 3 with Red*. 'That's the way I felt it. Why it affected me so, I don't know. It was born that way.'[10] 'I use colour in a sculpture when the image of my experience has colour in it.'[11] Perhaps unexpectedly for the rationalist commentator, he cites Van Gogh as a precursor whose colours 'had in his vision an existence and force all their own, independent of the object, and [who] also draws our attention to their psychological effect'.[12]

'Shapes, colours and lines speak their own language. They are events in themselves and in an organised construction they become beings – their psychological force is immediate, irresistible and universal to all species of mankind; not being the result of a convention as words are, they are unambiguous and it is, therefore, that their impact can influence the human psyche; it can break or mould it, it exults, it depresses, elates or makes desperate; it can bring order where there was confusion and it can disturb and exasperate where there was an order.'[13]

This was Gabo's experience of artistic language from the icon painters, who had found expressive freedom in the restriction to 'the basic elements of painting – lines, shapes, colours'[14]

3   **Face in a Headdress** c.1926
pencil and oil on paper
35.5 x 25.3 cm

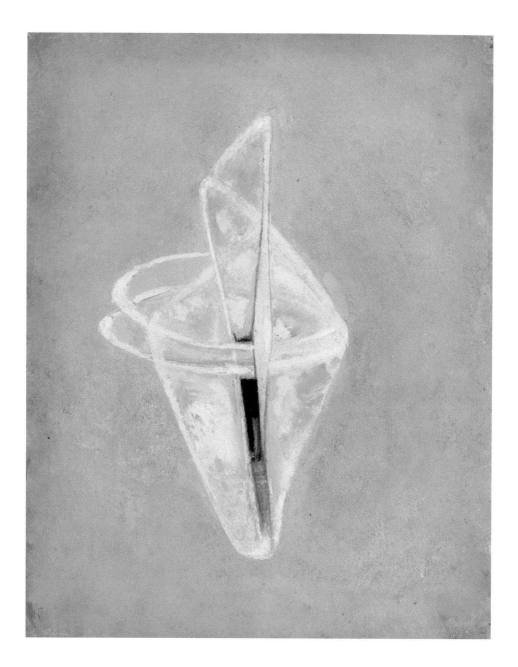

4   **Spinning** 1944
oil on paper mounted on board
19.5 x 15.5 cm

within the prescribed image, but more immediately from Vrubel and Matisse. It is no accident that Matisse's art came out of the studio of a Symbolist, Gustave Moreau, rather than Impressionism. In Symbolism colour as pigment took on that independent power for the first time in Western art since before the Renaissance. More than once in this exhibition, in *Face in a Headdress* (cat. no. 3) and *Study after Opus Two* (cat. no. 45), we are reminded of Odilon Redon, another Symbolist, who confronts us with the very stuff of colour. Gabo would never dissociate colour from its substance and so, if we return to 'The Realistic Manifesto', 'its light-absorbing material body', though hue was as important as tone. He would not try to paint white snow, white Carrara marble or a white chrysanthemum but for him each presented a different experience of white.

Not terribly successfully, and on one occasion at the cost of Miriam's blender, he attempted to grind lapis lazuli and other pigments to make his own paints and, quite probably, inks for the mono-print wood engravings, which he began to make in 1950.[15] These are monoprints because, rather than make a uniform edition, Gabo preferred to ink the block and burnish by hand each impression. In this way the full range of their normally single colour, from opacity to transparency, from thick to thin, could contribute to the spatial sensation of the carved drawing and the play between apparent solidity and the immaterial, and give the print its light.

Then what of the business of painting? Herbert Read, for one, was doubtful about oil paint as a constructive medium, but Nina recalls there always being a painting on the easel, though for almost ten years from 1945 to '54 it was generally the *Blue Kinetic Painting*, now in the Wadsworth Atheneum. It 'started out as a smallish rectangle, an upright rectangle, and then grew into a larger rectangle, and then a large circle, and then it was motorised. It turned very slowly.'[16] There were spates of painting, particularly in Cornwall during the war, in a studio borrowed from Peter Lanyon, and in the '60s in Connecticut when Miriam reported him 'deep in paintings which I suspect may be partly because he hasn't the energy for new sculptures.'[17]

A painting might be something to chew on in its own right but also a means of realising an image, conjured in the mind, which could not be resolved in sculpture, such as in the case of *Spinning*, 1944 (cat. no. 4): 'I often turn to painting when the image of my experience becomes so involved in structure, in form and in colour that there is no possible way for me to execute it in three-dimensional material. So when I cannot make it, I paint it on a two-dimensional surface.'[18]

Though still, in 1937, frustrated in his sculpture by the limitations of technology, Gabo came to recognise that the suggestion of movement, and hence time, could be just as effective in its impact as real, motorised movement and the same seems to apply to his sense of space. Again, it was not the actuality that counted but the experience of our consciousness. 'I am trying to show the penetration of space through everything.'[19] This was his constant theme and painting lent itself to it, perhaps encouraged by his friendships with Ben Nicholson and the young Peter Lanyon.

A colour could start as a line defining a shape, broaden into a plane and merge, absorbing and emanating light, into the expanses and depths of space, not as an illusion or an abstraction but as *Faktura* with an 'impact on our senses as real as the impact of light or an electric shock'.[20] 'A visual experience of colour is never flat, it is enveloped in light; and wherever light is there is space.'[21]

Several paintings are predominantly monochromatic, though a blue painting might contain the blues of many stones. *Embers* (cat. no. 27), begun in 1946 and not completed until 1960, is a painting of reds, invoking all our experience of the colour red. It is also a painting of light, of elisions and glazes, of coiling, transparent and dissolving forms. We are looking now beyond the surface of things into our visceral and psychological selves while descending to the centre of the earth and voyaging to the edge of space: the 'something cosmic' and 'the pulse of real life' that he so admired in his friend Mark Tobey's paintings.[22] Perhaps, in images such as this, unrealisable in three dimensions, we come closest to Gabo's innermost essence.

'Colour is the flesh of our visual perception of the world, not its skin.'[23]

Michael Harrison, Kettle's Yard, Cambridge
November 2003

Notes

1   Naum Gabo and Noton (Antoine) Pevsner, 'The Realistic Manifesto', Moscow, 5 August 1920, Gabo's translation.
2   Rackstraw Downes, 'Listening to Gabo', *Granta*, Cambridge, vol. lxvi, no. 1218, 19 May 1962.
3   *ibid*
4   Naum Gabo, *Of Divers Arts*, The A.W. Mellon Lectures in the Fine Arts, National Gallery of Art, Washington, 1959, Faber and Faber, London, 1962.
5   *op cit*, 'The Realistic Manifesto'.
6   *op cit*, 'The Realistic Manifesto'.
7   *op cit*, *Of Divers Arts*, II.
8   *ibid*
9   *op cit*, *Of Divers Arts*, II.
10 A.L. Chanin, 'Gabo Makes a Construction', *Art News*, New York, vol. 52, no. 7, 1953.
11 Katherine Kuh, *The Artist's Voice: Talks with Seventeen Artists*, Harper and Row, New York, 1962.
12 *op cit*, *Of Divers Arts*, IV.
13 Naum Gabo, 'On Constructive Realism', Trowbridge Lecture, Yale University, 19 March 1948, published in K.S. Dreier, J.J. Sweeney and N. Gabo, *Three Lectures on Modern Art*, Philosophical Library, New York, 1949.
14 Naum Gabo, 'The Concepts of Russian Art', *World Review*, London, June 1942.
15 His son-in-law, Graham Williams, is all but certain that only commercially made inks were eventually used in the monoprints.
16 Nina Williams recorded by Graham Williams, 2003.
17 Quoted in Martin Hammer and Christina Lodder, *Constructing Modernity: The Art & Career of Naum Gabo*, Yale University Press, New Haven & London, 2000, p.441.
18 *op cit*, *The Artist's Voice*.
19 *ibid*
20 *op cit*, 'On Constructive Realism'
21 *op cit*, *Of Divers Arts*, IV.
22 Naum Gabo, 'Mark Tobey', catalogue, Galerie Beyeler, Basel, 1970.
23 *ibid*

All quotations of Naum Gabo, except those from *Of Divers Arts*, may be found in Martin Hammer and Christina Lodder, *Gabo on Gabo*, Artists Bookworks, Sussex, 2002.

5 **Study for Head No.2** 1915
blue pencil on paper
18 x 11 cm

6   **Self Portrait** c.1907-10
oil on canvas
56 x 47.5 cm

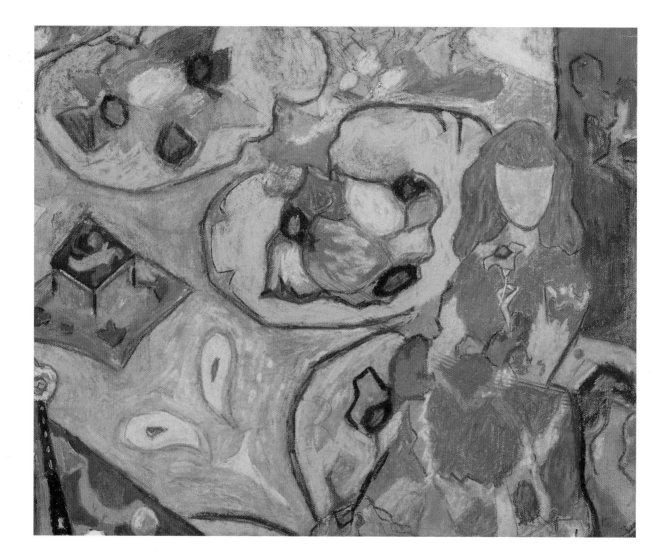

7 **Christmas** c.1910-12
pastel on paper
36.3 x 45 cm

8   **Hamlet** 1912
pencil and watercolour on paper
14.2 x 11 cm

9   **Ballerina** c.1926-27
pencil and paint on board
10.2 x 7.7 cm

10 **Costume Sketch for 'La Chatte'** 1926
pencil and pastel on paper
28 x 22.5 cm

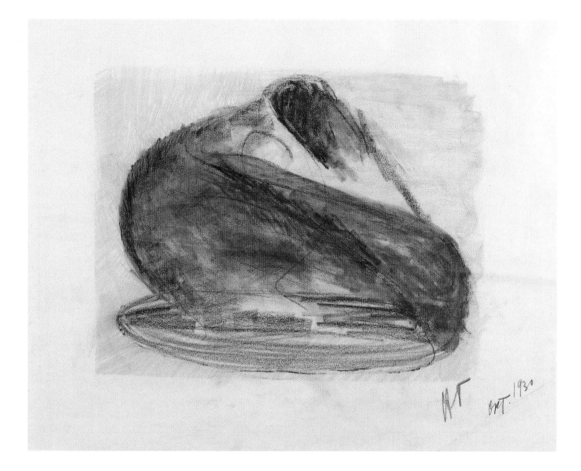

11 **Sketch for a Carving in Stone** 1930
crayon and gouache on paper
33 x 48 cm

12 **Untitled**
crayon and pencil on paper
14.5 x 17.5 cm

13 **Sketch for a Stone Carving** 1933
pencil and crayon on paper
17.3 x 15.2 cm

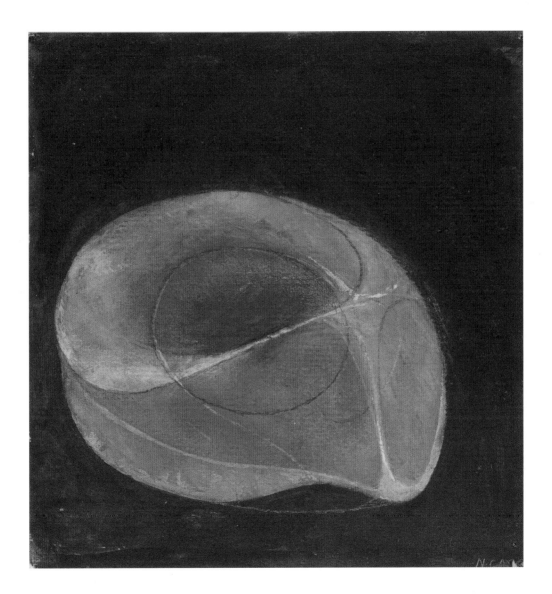

14 **Untitled** c.1930s
gouache and pencil on paper
13.5 x 13.5 cm

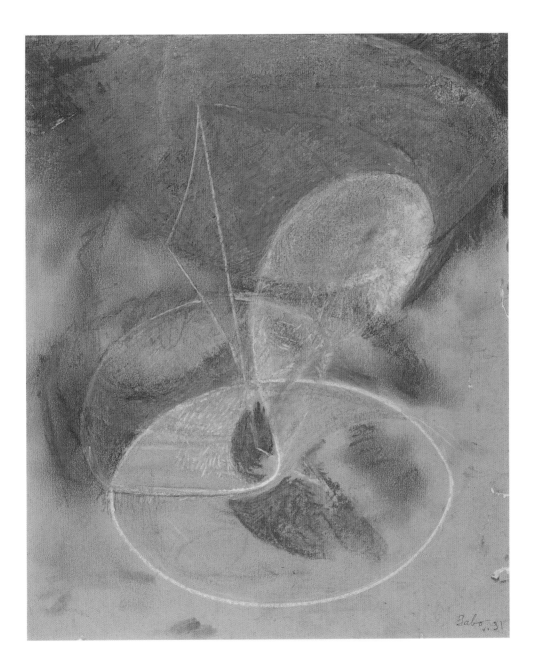

15 **Construction for a Pond** 1931
pastel and watercolour on paper
21.8 x 18 cm

16 **Painting in Browns**
oil on paper on composition panel
14.6 x 17.3 cm

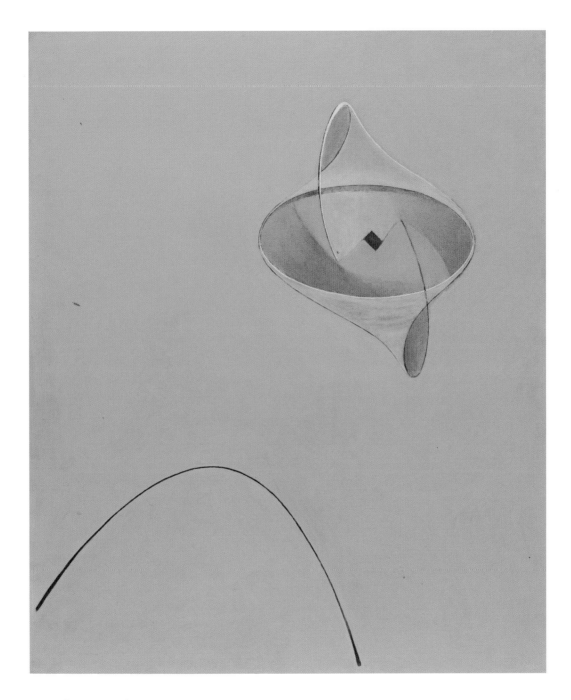

17 **Hovering** 1940/1970s
oil on photographic paper on board
76 x 63.5 cm

18 **Abstract Painting** c.1940
oil, gouache, pastel, crayon and pencil on card
19 x 14.5 cm

19 **Turquoise – Kinetic Painting** 1945
   oil on board mounted on a motorised black perspex revolving disc
   diameter 43 cm

20 **Untitled** c.1950s
pencil and paint on card
19 x 26.5 cm

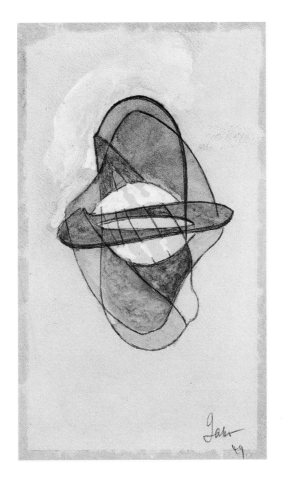

21 **Drawing for Opus Three** 1949
pencil and gouache on paper
20 x 13 cm

22 **Opus Seven** c.1955
monoprint from an engraved wood block
23.3 x 26.7 cm

23 **Opus One** 1950
monoprint from an engraved wood block
17.5 x 15.5 cm

24 **Two Images Interlocked** 1954/55
oil on board
46.5 x 39.5 cm

25 **The Field of Asphodels** 1960
oil on paper
19.4 x 16.8 cm

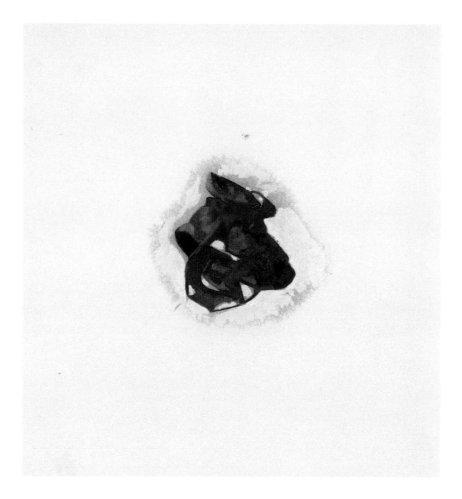

26 **Dark Blue Oil Sketch** 1960
oil on paper
28 x 23 cm

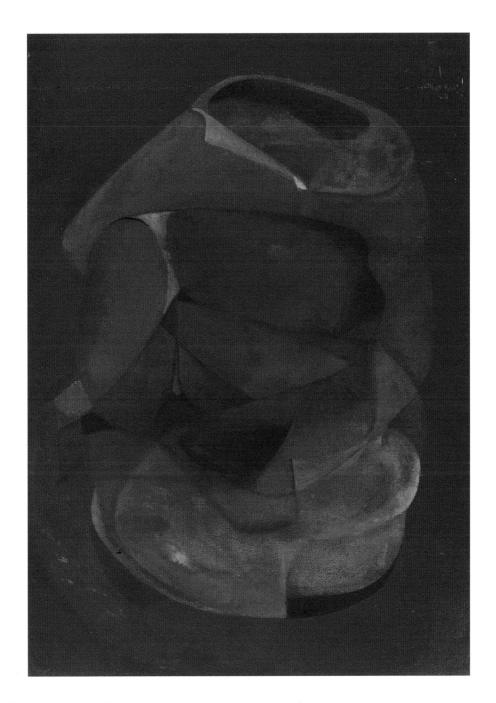

27 **Embers** c.1960
oil on board
84.5 x 61 cm

28 **Opus Six** 1955/56
monoprint from an engraved wood block
42 x 35 cm

29 **Opus Nine** 1970s
monoprint from an engraved wood block
32 x 35.6 cm

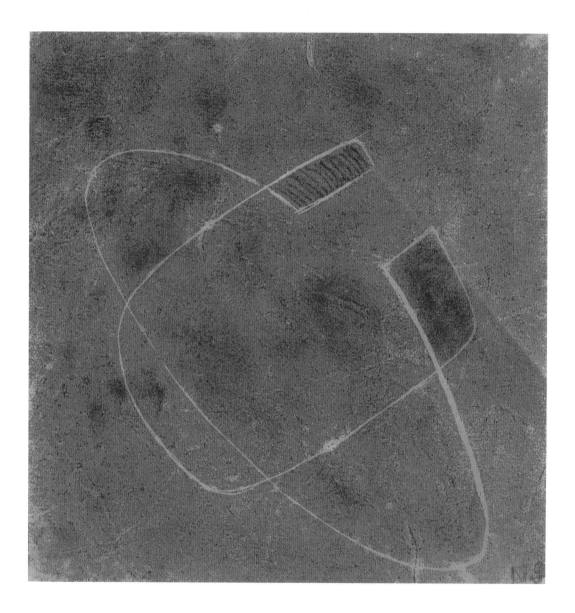

30 **WE 24**
monoprint from an engraved wood block printed on yellow paper
14.8 x 14 cm

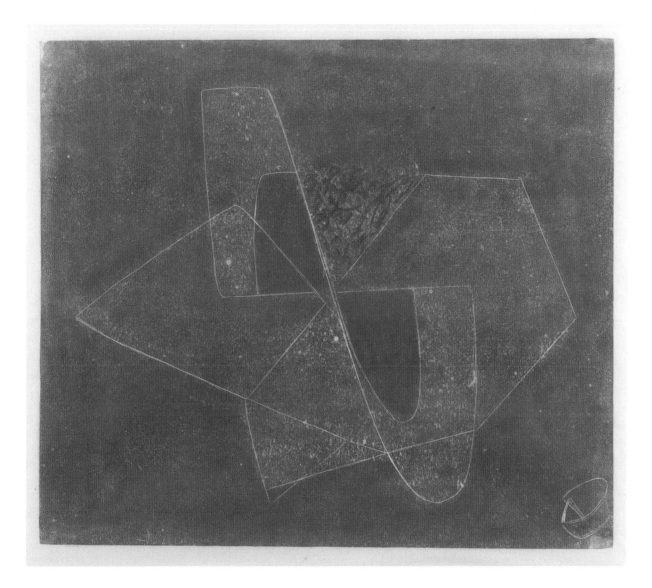

31 **Opus Ten** 1960s
monoprint from an engraved wood block
43 x 51 cm

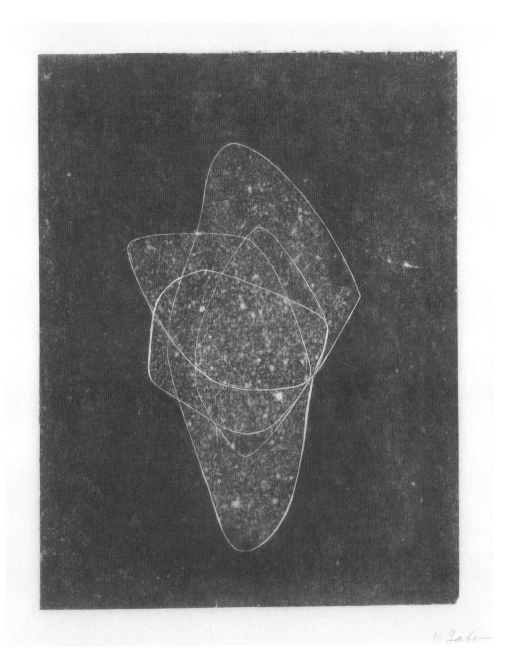

32 **Opus Eight** 1960s
monoprint from an engraved wood block
45.5 x 39.8 cm

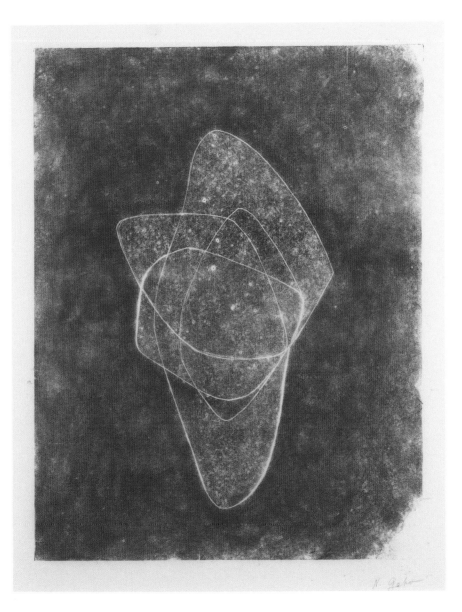

33 **Opus Eight** 1970s
monoprint from an engraved wood block
33.5 x 27 cm

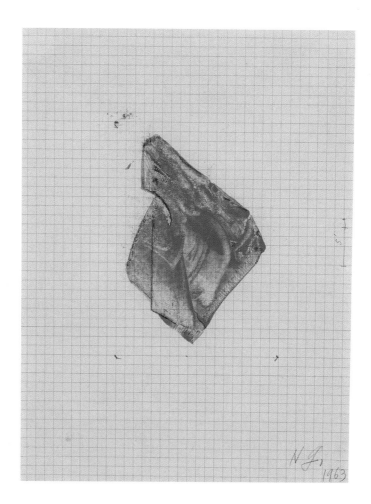

34 **Sketch for Blue Lithograph** 1963
oil and pencil on graph paper
19.4 x 14.6 cm

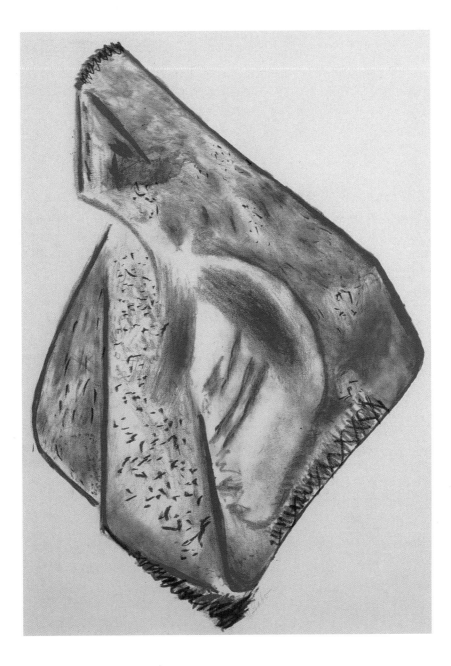

35 **Blue Lithograph** 1960s
lithograph
45.7 x 31.9 cm

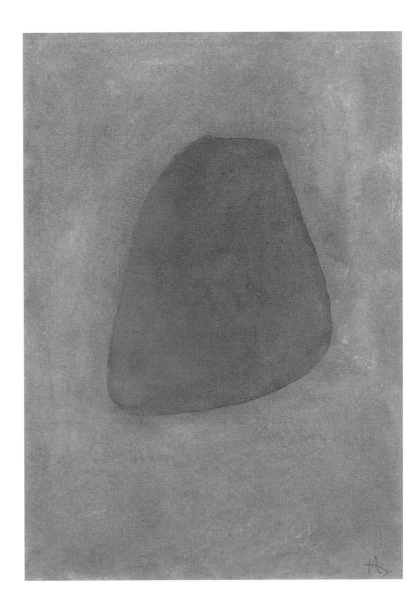

36 **Oil Sketch** 1960s
oil on paper
26.5 x 19 cm

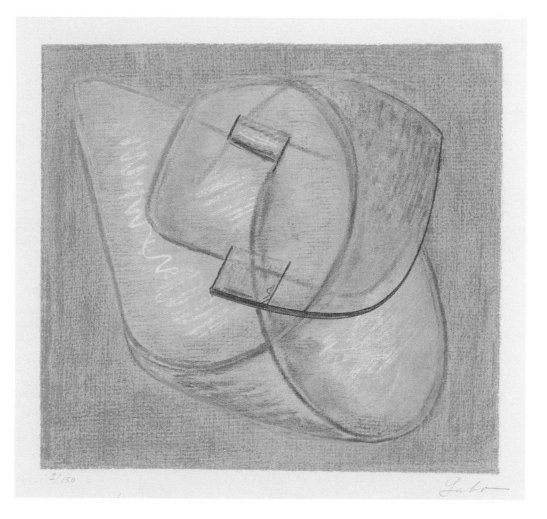

2/150

Gabo

37 **Green Lithograph** 1960-61
lithograph, edition of 150
28 x 23 cm

38 Untitled 1960-65
oil on paper
28 x 24.5 cm

39 **Opus Eight** 1960s
monoprint from an engraved wood block
46.5 x 39.5 cm

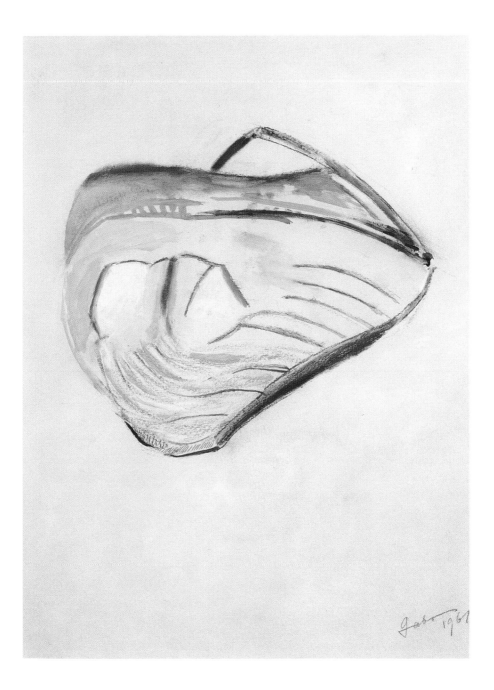

40 **Oil Sketch** 1961
oil and pencil on paper
38.4 x 28.6 cm

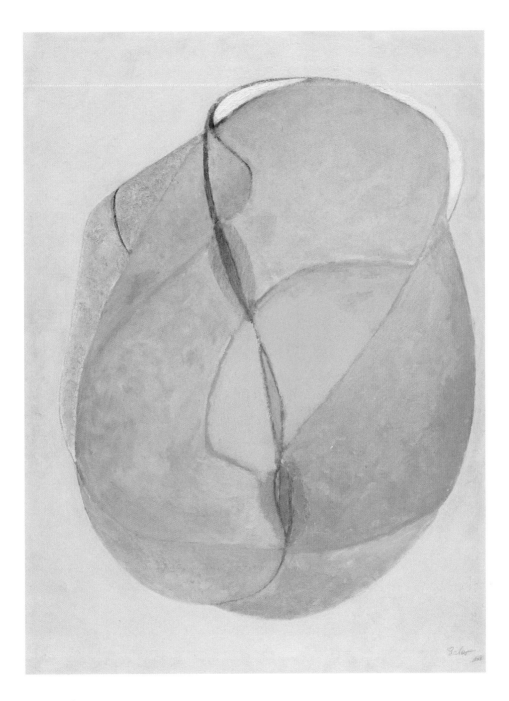

41 **Enclosed Space** 1968
oil on board
67.5 x 50.2 cm

42 **Untitled**
oil on emery paper
28 x 22.7 cm

43 **Oil Sketch** 1960s-70s
oil on paper
23.5 x 18.5 cm

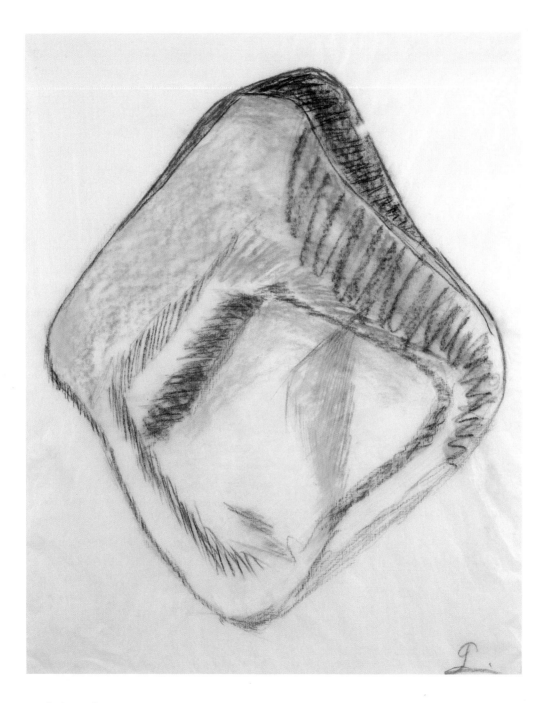

44 **Study in Colour** c.1960-70s
pastel and crayon on tracing paper
55.6 x 45.3 cm

45 **Study after Opus Two**
pencil and oil on paper
26.7 x 19 cm

46 **Untitled (red, yellow, blue)** 1973/75
stencil print
32.2 x 27.9 cm

47 **Untitled** 1970s
oil and pencil on paper, partly created with stencils
57.8 x 48.4 cm

48 **Fog** 1970s
lithograph, edition of 50
42 x 37.5 cm

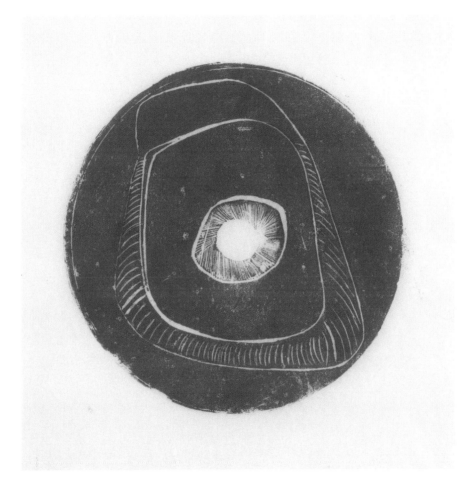

49 **Opus Twelve** 1965/68
monoprint from an engraved wood block
26.5 x 20 cm

50 **The Loop** 1970s
monoprint from an engraved wood block reworked with oil and pastels
43 x 42 cm

51 **Opus Ten** 1970s
monoprint from an engraved wood block
33.3 x 38 cm

52 **Untitled (red, yellow, blue)** 1973/75
stencil print
41 x 30 cm

53 **Oval Form** 1970s
monoprint from an engraved wood block reworked with oil and pastels
30.5 x 24.5 cm

54-57 **Oval Forms** 1970s
monoprints from an engraved wood block reworked with oil and pastels
each approx: 30 x 24 cm

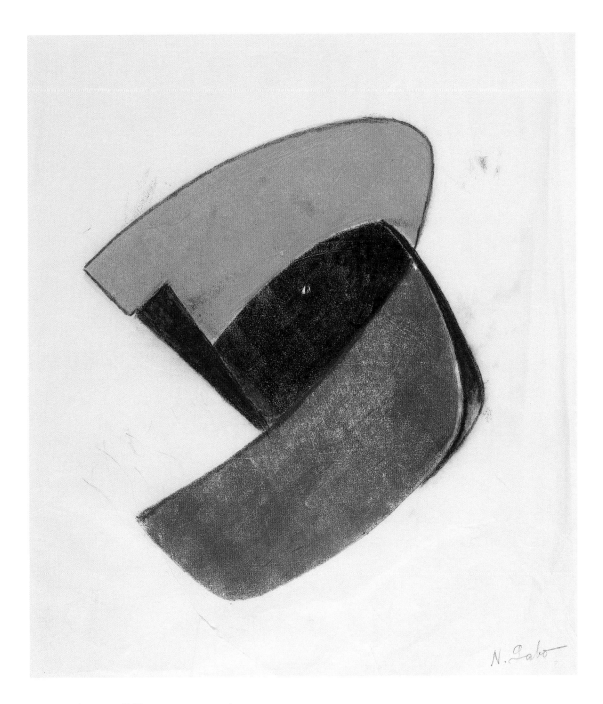

59 **Design for Portfolio Cover** 1970/73
stencil print with added crayon and paint
58.6 x 49.2 cm

60 **Untitled** 1972-73
stencil print with added crayon and paint
62 x 46.5 cm

61 **Untitled (red, yellow, blue)** 1973/75
stencil print
41 x 30.5 cm

62 **Nina's Painting** 1973
oil on paper on board
22 x 22 cm

Biography

1890	Born Briansk, Russia. Named Naum Neemia Pevsner. He had four brothers, including Alexei and Antoine, and two sisters.
1910	Graduated from Gymnasium at Kursk. Enrolled in medical faculty at Munich University.
1910-14	In Munich.
1911	Transferred to study of natural sciences.
1912	Studied engineering at Technische Hochschule, Munich. During these years attended Professor Wölfflin's lectures on the History of Art. First visit to Paris.
1913	Walking tour through Italy from Munich to Florence and Venice.
1913-14	Visited brother Antoine who was painting in Paris.
1914	At outbreak of war went to Copenhagen, Bergen, and then Oslo with younger brother Alexei.
1915	Made first constructions using the name Gabo. December: joined by elder brother Antoine.
1917	April: returned to Russia.
1918-20	Worked on constructions and taught unofficially at State Free Art Studios. Project for a radio station at Serpukhov.
1920	First public exhibition in the open air on Tverskoi Boulevard, Moscow. Wrote *Realistic Manifesto*, published in Moscow, which was also signed by brother Antoine. First construction with motor.
1922	Left Moscow for Berlin. Helped to install and exhibited in the *Erste Russische Kunstausstellung*, organised by the Soviet Government at the Galerie van Diemen, Berlin. Project for a Monument for an Observatory.
1922-32	Lived and worked in Berlin.
1924	Exhibited at the Galerie Percier, Paris: *Constructivistes Russes: Gabo et Pevsner* and was included in *Societé Anonyme* Russian Exhibition in New York.
1924-25	Project for a Monument for an Airport.
1925	Project for a Monument for an Institute of Physics and Mathematics.
1926	Exhibited in America at the Little Review Gallery, New York, with van Doesburg and Pevsner. Began work on *La Chatte*.
1927	April 30, first performance of *La Chatte* at the Casino Theatre in Monte Carlo with sets, costumes and properties designed and executed by Gabo with assistance from Pevsner (the production also travelled to Paris, London and Berlin).
1928	Lectured at Bauhaus. Published article, 'Gestaltung?' in the periodical *Bauhaus* vol. 2 no. 4.
1929	Project for a *Fête Lumière* for the Brandenburg Gate, Berlin.
1930	First one-man exhibition of constructions at the Kestner-Gesellschaft, Hanover.
1931	Project for the Palace of the Soviets Competition.

1932	Left Germany for Paris. Project for a Monument for an Airport.
1932-35	Member of the group *Abstraction-Création*.
1935	First visit to England. Exhibited in Hartford Conn. with Pevsner, Domela and Mondrian.
1936	Exhibited with fifteen artists in *Abstract and Concrete* at the Lefèvre Gallery, London. Exhibited with Pevsner at the Chicago Arts Club. Seven works included in *Cubism and Abstract Art* at the Museum of Modern Art, New York. Settled in London. Married Miriam Israels in London.
1937	Edited with J. L. Martin and Ben Nicholson Circle: *International Survey of Constructive Art*. Two works included in large Constructivist exhibition at the Kunsthalle, Basel, and two in Constructivist exhibition at the London Gallery, London. Participated in exhibition in Jeu de Paume, Paris.
1938	One-man exhibition at the London Gallery, London. Visited the United States: exhibited at the Wadsworth Atheneum, Hartford, at the Julien Levy Gallery, New York and at Vassar College, Poughkeepsie.
1939	At outbreak of war moved to Carbis Bay, Cornwall. Exhibited one work in the San Francisco Golden Gate exhibition, another in Toledo, Ohio, two in Guggenheim Jeune, London, one in Museum of Modern Art, New York, more than one in Galerie Charpentier, Paris.
1941	Birth of daughter Nina Serafima.
1942	Exhibited in *New Movements in Art. Contemporary Work in England*, London Museum, London, Leicester Museum, *Societé Anonyme*, New Haven.
1943-44	Worked with Design Research Unit, London. Produced an advanced design for a car for Jowett which did not go into production.
1946	Left England for the United States.
1948	Exhibited with Pevsner at the Museum of Modern Art, New York. Lectured at Museum of Modern Art and at Yale and Chicago Institute of Design.
1949	Commissioned to design sculptures for lobbies of the Esso Building, Rockefeller Center, New York (project never carried out). Participated in *Les Premières maîtres de l'art abstrait* organised by Michael Seuphor at Galerie Maeght, Paris.
1950	Commissioned to make construction for the Sadie A. May wing of the Baltimore Museum of Art. Exhibited and lectured at Baltimore Museum of Art.
1951	Baltimore construction completed and installed. Exhibition at the Massachusetts Institute of Technology.
1952	Became a citizen of the United States of America. Exhibition, with Josef Albers, at the Chicago Arts Club.
1953	One-man exhibition at the Pierre Matisse Gallery, New York. Exhibition, with Alexander Calder, at the Wadsworth Atheneum, Hartford. Awarded second prize in the *Unknown Political Prisoner*, international sculpture competition.
1953-54	Professor at Harvard University Graduate School of Architecture.

1954	Awarded Guggenheim Fellowship. Awarded Mr and Mrs Frank G. Logan Medal of the Art Institute of Chicago.
1954-55	Commissioned to make sculpture for the Bijenkorf Building in Rotterdam.
1956	Commissioned to make bas-relief for the US Rubber Company, Rockefeller Center, New York. Completed in November.
1957	Bijenkorf construction, 85 feet high, completed and installed. Publication of Gabo book by Lund Humphries.
1958	One-man exhibition, Boymans Museum, Rotterdam and Stedelijk Museum, Amsterdam.
1959	Delivered A. W. Mellon Lectures, Washington D.C. Brother Alexei re-discovered Gabo through an exhibition catalogue.
1960	Prize from the Brandeis University.
1961	Participated in exhibitions of kinetic art held at the Stedelijk Museum, Amsterdam, and at the Moderna Museet, Stockholm.
1962	Visited brothers Mark, Jeremy and Alexei, and sister Anna, in Moscow and Leningrad. Antoine Pevsner died.
1964	Publication of Alexei Pevsner's book on his brothers Gabo and Pevsner.
1965	Elected member of the National Institute of Art and Letters.
1965-66	Retrospective exhibition at the Stedelijk Museum, Amsterdam; the Kunsthalle Mannheim; the Wilhelm-Lehmbruck-Museum, Duisburg; the Kunsthaus Zurich; the Moderna Museet, Stockholm; the Tate Gallery, London.
1966	Elected to Royal Academy of Arts, Sweden.
1967	Awarded Honorary Doctorate at Royal College of Art, London. Awarded Grosse Kunstpreis des Landes Nordrhein-Westfalen.
1968	Retrospective exhibition at Albright-Knox Art Gallery, Buffalo, New York. Alexei Pevsner visited Gabo in America.
1969	Elected to the American Academy of Arts and Sciences.
1970	Commissioned to make *Torsion* fountain, installed at St. Thomas's Hospital in 1975.
1970-72	Travelling Exhibition: Louisiana Museet, Humlebaek, Denmark; Sonia Henje Museum Høxikodden, Norway; Nasjonalgalereit, Oslo; Nationalgalerie, Berlin; Kunstverein, Hanover; Musée de Peinture et Sculpture, Grenoble; Musée National d'Art Moderne, Paris; Gulbenkian Foundation, Lisbon. Alexei Pevsner visited Gabo in London.
1971	Made an Honorary K.B.E.
1973	Commissioned to make sculpture for the Nationalgalerie, Berlin.
1975	Elected to 50-member American Academy of Arts and Letters.
1976	November 16, opening of St. Thomas's Hospital and inauguration of *Torsion* fountain by Queen Elizabeth II.
1976-77	November - January. One-man exhibition at the Tate Gallery, London.
1977	August 23, died in Waterbury (Connecticut) Hospital after a long illness.

ISBN   1-904621-01-5

Photographs: Ian Parker
Catalogue © Annely Juda Fine Art 2003
All works © Nina Williams
Text © Michael Harrison 2003
Printed by BAS Printers Ltd, England